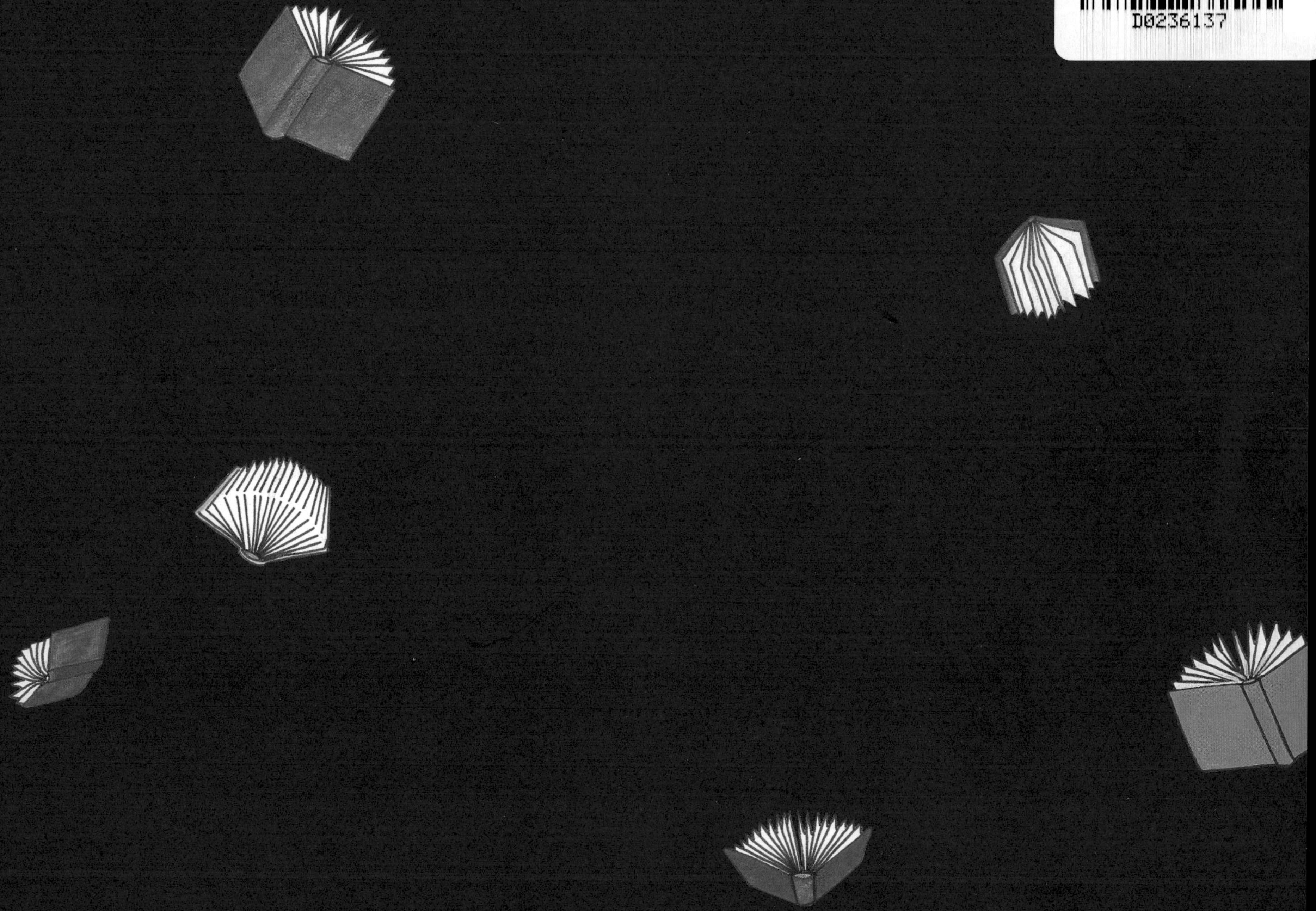

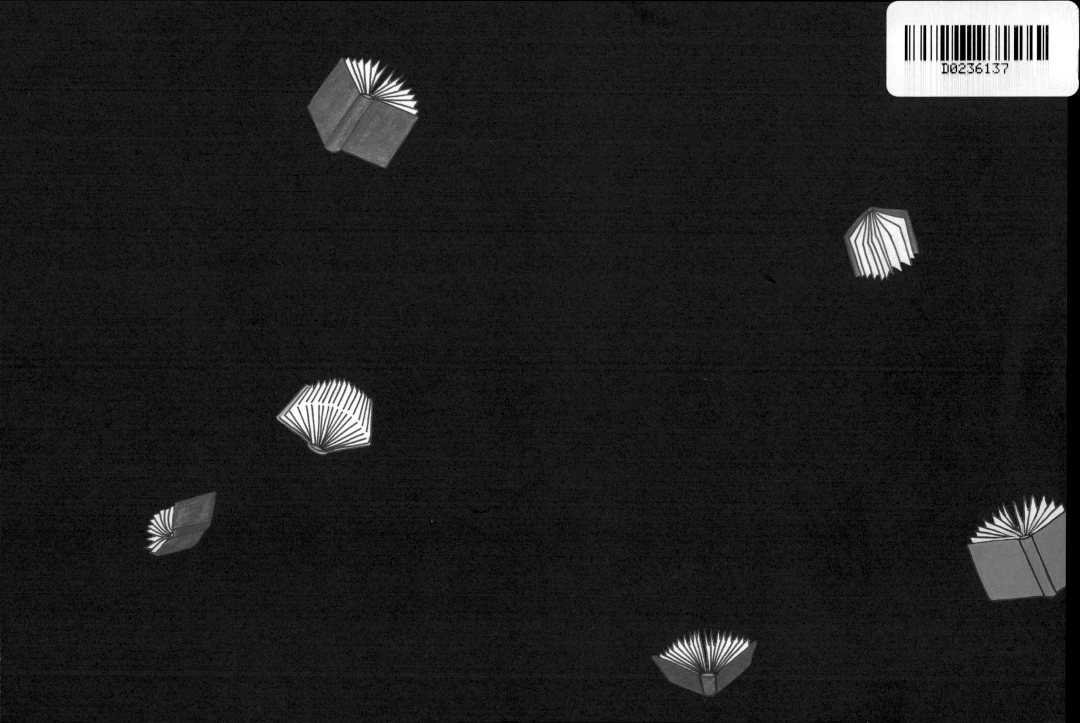

THE NIGHT BOOKMOBILE

Audrey Niffenegger

JONATHAN CAPE

LONDON

The first time I saw the Night Bookmobile, I was walking down Ravenswood Avenue at four o'clock in the morning. It was late in the summer, at that quiet time of morning when the cicadas have given up but the birds haven't started in yet. I'd been walking for about an hour. I had started at Belmont and then I was at Irving Park Road. There are two trains that run along Ravenswood, the Chicago-Northwestern and the Ravenswood El, and periodically one of them would run up behind me and ahead of me with nobody in it. I was starting to feel a little peaceful, a little tired, so I kept on walking.

Everything was very clean and slightly wet, because it had been raining around three, which is when Richard and I had had the argument. So I was out walking around in the cool end of the night, and I saw the Night Bookmobile.

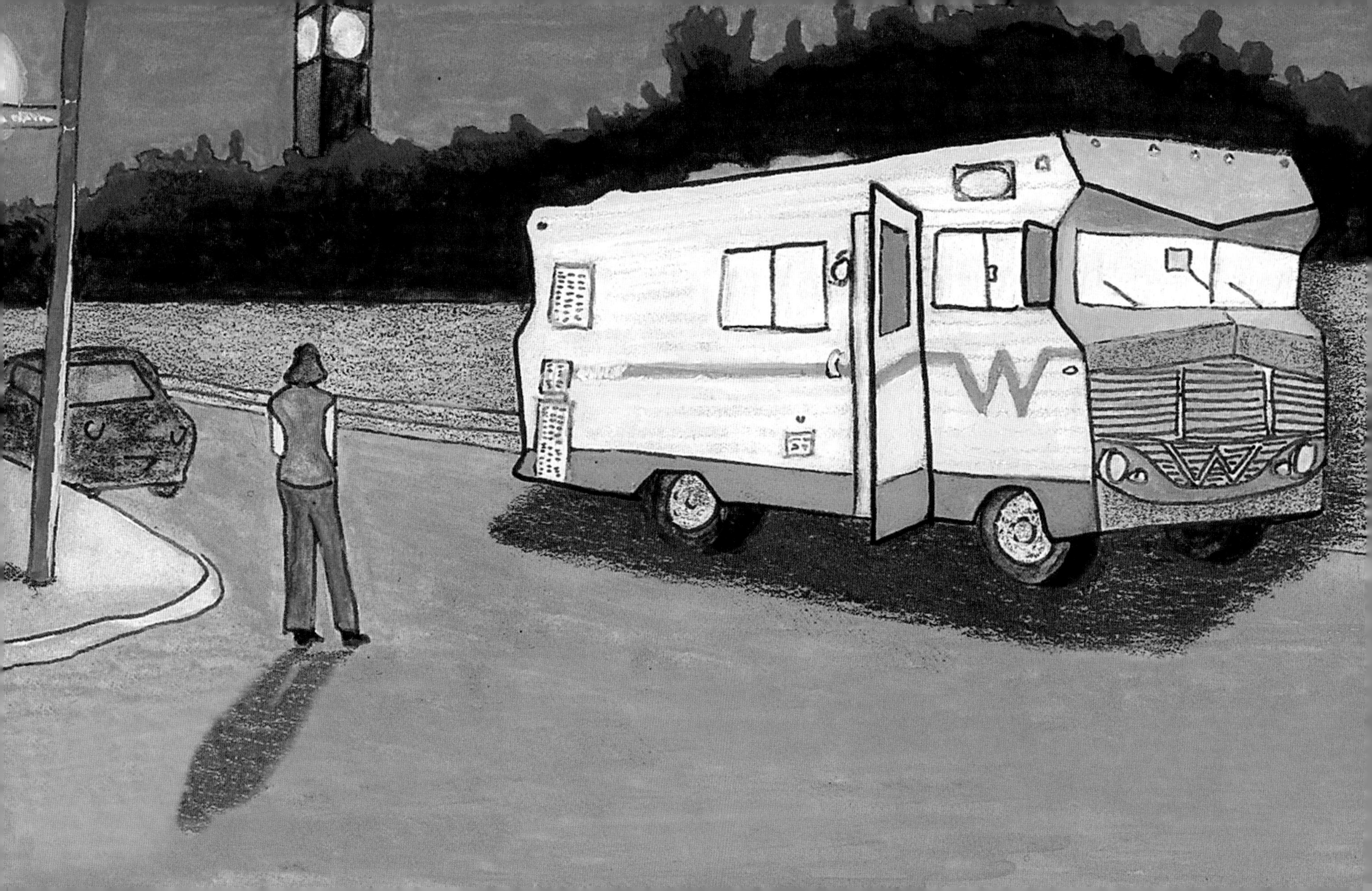

It was sitting at the corner of Ravenswood and Belle Plaine. I didn't know it was the Night Bookmobile, of course. It was an enormous, battered Winnebago, all lit up and thumping out "I Shot the Sheriff."

I like Bob Marley as well as the next person, but there was something pretty peculiar, almost scary, about hearing it played really loud on a deserted Chicago street at that hour.

I paused infinitesimally, but I didn't want whoever was in the Winnebago to think that I was pausing because of them, so I started walking again.

The door was open, and I glanced in.

I must have been staring at him, because he looked at me over his bifocals and said,

Would you like to see the collection?

Now you might be wondering if it was at all safe for a woman like me, not very tall, not very old, not a black belt in karate, to be wandering around alone like this in the wee hours. All I can say is at that time in my life I used to do it a lot, and no one ever bothered me. So when the old gentleman inquired whether I cared to see the collection, instead of shaking my head and continuing on, which is what any sensible girl would have done, I said,

What collection?

The Night Bookmobile?

THE NIGHT BOOKMOBILE
THE LIBRARY
ROBERT OPENSHAW,
LIBRARIAN
Hours: Dusk to Dawn

At your service.

Mr. Openshaw made a sort-of-pretend bow and turned off the music.

I stepped up into the Winnebago and past him, and peered into the back of the camper.

The Night Bookmobile seemed larger from the inside—much larger. The lighting was subdued and pleasant. The whole place smelled of old, dry paper, with a little whiff of wet dog, which I like. I looked back at the librarian. He was reading his newspaper.

I turned to the books. The section I was standing in was full of children's books. I drifted along, noticing text-books mingled with picture books, and an assortment of books you don't usually see in libraries: family Bibles,

photo albums, telephone books. Some of the books had catalog numbers on their spines, some didn't. The books weren't arranged by subject, and some of the numbers seemed to belong to different systems. In fact, the

books seemed to belong to many different libraries. I wondered if Mr. Openshaw was running around stealing books from all these places and putting them in his Winnebago.

I moved farther along the aisle. Then I noticed something strange, which was that every book on the shelves was familiar.

That is, I had read all the books. I mean, I'm a pretty avid reader, but I had never been anywhere, even my own apartment, where I'd read everything. *Everything.*

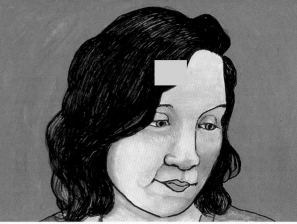

From Jane Austen to Paul Auster, from *Betty Crocker's Cookbook* to *The Raw and the Cooked* to my college biology textbook, every book on the shelves was familiar.

I even saw a lot of books I'd forgotten I'd read, Judy Blumes and Agatha Christies.

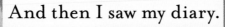

And then I saw my diary.

"This is mine!"

"Huh?" "They're all yours."

I took it off the shelf and opened it. On the first page was the date, December 25, 1976. "Dear Diary, Hello. I am at Grandma Eloise's, it is Christmas . . . " Over my painstaking purple-ballpoint-pen handwriting was stamped THE LIBRARY. I walked back to Mr. Openshaw.

"This collection consists of all the books you've ever read. We also have all the periodicals and ephemera — cereal boxes and such — which are in Section C, to your right."

"It's a very complete collection."

"But how — were you waiting for me?"

"No, not exactly."

"You see, the Library, in its entirety, comprises all the printed matter ever read by anyone alive at this moment. So we are quite ready for any patron."

"But—"

Suddenly a bell rang.

"I'm afraid the Library is now closed. "Hours: Dusk to Dawn," you know."

He took the diary from me and replaced it on the shelf.

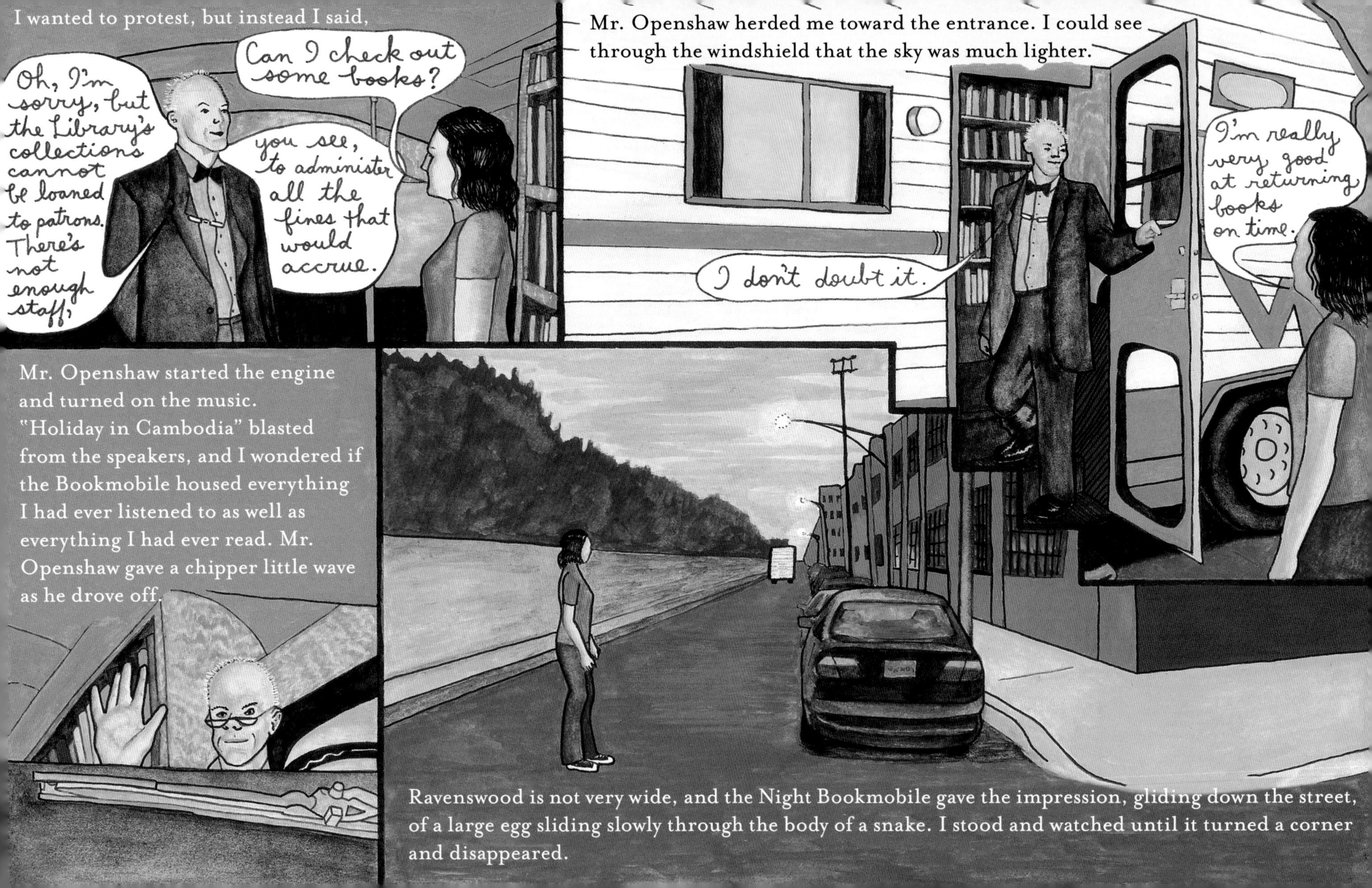

I wanted to protest, but instead I said,
Can I check out some books?
Oh, I'm sorry, but the Library's collections cannot be loaned to patrons. There's not enough staff,
you see, to administer all the fines that would accrue.
Mr. Openshaw herded me toward the entrance. I could see through the windshield that the sky was much lighter.
I'm really very good at returning books on time.
I don't doubt it.
Mr. Openshaw started the engine and turned on the music. "Holiday in Cambodia" blasted from the speakers, and I wondered if the Bookmobile housed everything I had ever listened to as well as everything I had ever read. Mr. Openshaw gave a chipper little wave as he drove off.
Ravenswood is not very wide, and the Night Bookmobile gave the impression, gliding down the street, of a large egg sliding slowly through the body of a snake. I stood and watched until it turned a corner and disappeared.

The sun was shining as I let myself into our apartment. I stood in front of my bookshelves and there were all my books, haphazardly crowded together as always, needing dusting, as always. I was running my finger across my broken-backed set of *The Lord of the Rings* when Richard appeared in the doorway of our bedroom. He had gone to sleep in his clothes. He stood blinking at the sunlight. Somehow I always loved him best after a fight, and right then I couldn't even remember what we'd been fighting about.

So I told him.

And he didn't.

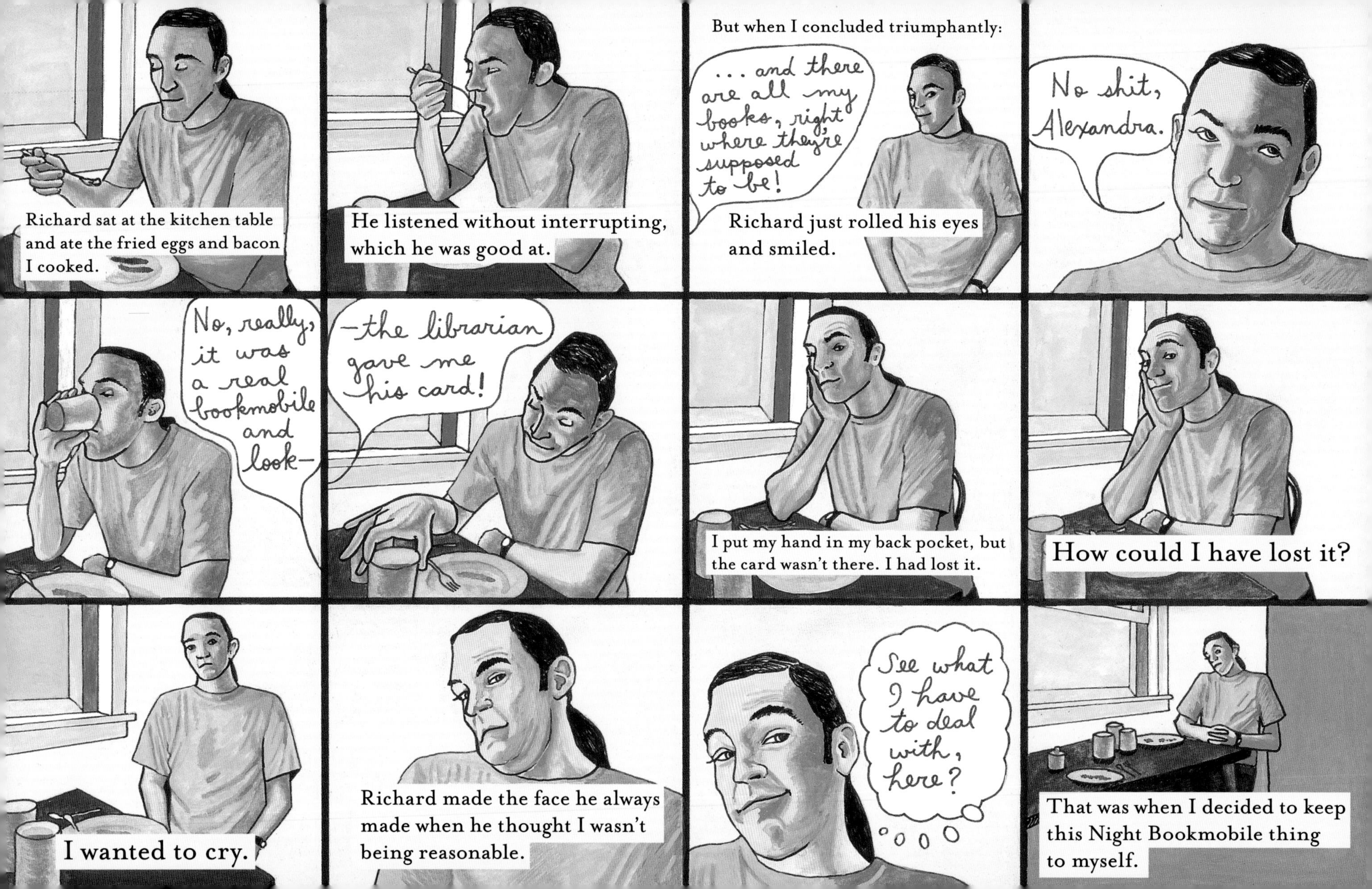
Richard sat at the kitchen table and ate the fried eggs and bacon I cooked.
He listened without interrupting, which he was good at.
But when I concluded triumphantly:
... and there are all my books, right where they're supposed to be!
Richard just rolled his eyes and smiled.
No shit, Alexandra.
No, really, it was a real bookmobile and look—
—the librarian gave me his card!
I put my hand in my back pocket, but the card wasn't there. I had lost it.
How could I have lost it?
I wanted to cry.
Richard made the face he always made when he thought I wasn't being reasonable.
See what I have to deal with, here?
That was when I decided to keep this Night Bookmobile thing to myself.

Have you ever found your heart's desire and then lost it? I had seen myself, a portrait of myself as a reader. My childhood: hours spent in airless classrooms, days home sick from school reading Nancy Drew, forbidden books read secretively late at night. Teenage years reading—trying to read—books I'd heard were important, *Naked Lunch* and *The Fountainhead*, *Ulysses* and *Women in Love* . . . It was as though I had dreamt the perfect lover, who vanished as I woke, leaving me pining and surly.

I went back the next night. I stood at the corner of Ravenswood and Belle Plaine for six hours, by myself. I brought a book with me, *The Moonstone*, by Wilkie Collins. I'd read it a few times, so I figured it would already be in the collection and I could compare the copies. When the sun came up I went home.

I waited at the corner of Ravenswood and Belle Plaine more times than I can count. Then I gave up looking for the Bookmobile on that particular corner and began roaming the city aimlessly at night. Richard accused me of seeing someone else, and I couldn't convince him otherwise. He moved out. I found myself alone in my apartment, alone with my books.

I began reading all the time. On the El, on my lunch hour, during every meal, I read. I looked forward to finding each book again someday on the shelves of the Bookmobile. I wondered if Mr. Openshaw was impressed with my choices, and my dedication. Like a pregnant woman eating for two, I read for myself and the librarian.

Years passed.

The second time I saw the Night Bookmobile, it was another chance encounter. I was walking down Clark Street, past Wrigley Field. It was only ten o'clock or so on a beautiful May night, and a baseball game had just finished. The Night Bookmobile stood right there in the McDonald's parking lot—in the midst of swarming Cubs fans—playing "Rock Lobster" by the B-52's at top volume. No one paid any attention at all.

I ran toward it, elbowing and shoving my way through the crowd.

Mr. Openshaw was reading a tiny pamphlet, which I thought might be one of those *Watchtower* things the Jehovah's Witnesses hand out.

I rapped on the window, and he glanced up, startled . . .

and then swung the door open with a smile.

Mr. Openshaw!
Alexandra! What a pleasure!
I can't believe — I've been trying to find you! I waited and waited!
I stepped up and he shut the door and turned down the music.
Tea?
Yes, please.
I realized that I was waving my hands and talking too loudly.
Now then. I'm sorry I haven't been up this way — how long has it been?
Mr. Openshaw got up and disappeared into a tiny alcove behind the driver's seat.
Almost nine years.
Oh, dear. I do usually get around a bit faster than that. I'm afraid there has been a
shortage of staff — budget cuts, you know. The Library seems to think we can do everything on
the Internet now, but of course it really just makes more work.
But here we are! Would you like a cookie with your tea?
Sure.

All this time I had been sneaking glances at the books. I wasn't quite sure, but there did seem to be a whole new aisle at the back. I hesitated.

Mr. Openshaw?

Yes, dear?

I was wondering—?

Indeed?

I want to stay here. I want to come with you. I could be your assistant...

Mr. Openshaw paused and considered.

Unfortunately, Alexandra, that isn't possible. Not that I don't appreciate your kind offer.

I'm really very sorry.

Would you care to use the collection tonight? You've made many fine acquisitions since we last met.

I nodded. I could hardly see through the tears that welled in my eyes. I set my teacup on the card catalog and stumbled toward the back of the Bookmobile.

Here was consolation. I wiped my nose on the back of my hand and surveyed the shelves. In the same way that perfume captures the essence of a flower, these shelves of books were a distillation of my life. Here was *A Distant Mirror*, by Barbara Tuchman, which I remembered reading in a coffee shop while waiting for a blind date who never showed up. Here was my paperback copy of *Anna Karenina*, fattened by repeated reading. I picked up *Gravity's Rainbow*. As I fanned through the book I saw that the text stopped at page fifty-seven; the remaining pages were blank. I had never finished reading it. A popsicle stick served to mark the place I had not come back to.

I spent the night roaming the stacks. Mr. Openshaw stayed at the wheel of the Bookmobile, reading. I was looking through a blue book about a girl who wouldn't take off her cowboy hat when I heard the bell. It was dawn. I walked down the main aisle and stood silently behind Mr. Openshaw. He was reading an instruction manual for a clock radio. Our eyes met in the rearview mirror.

I climbed down and watched as the Night Bookmobile convulsed into motion and made its way down Clark Street, spewing Jimi Hendrix. I knew what I had to do.

I went to library school. I drove out to the suburbs four nights a week and sat through classes on cataloging, patron relations, and the latest information storage and retrieval technologies. During the day I waitressed, and read. I wondered if Mr. Openshaw knew what I was up to. I imagined shelves and shelves of books with titles like *The Dewey Decimal System and You* and figured he probably did.

I graduated from library school and got a job as a reference librarian at the Sulzer branch of the Chicago Public Library. It was a new library, sunny and crowded with small children and patrons who needed to know the names of Civil War generals and where to get tax forms. I liked working in a place where people came to read in public. I imagined their Bookmobiles, each collection growing as its reader read. Once again, I began to wander the streets of Chicago at dusk.

Of course I found it when I wasn't looking for it. Perhaps it was looking for me. I was walking down Western Avenue, on my way to the Empty Bottle to hear a band and have a few drinks with a friend on a dismal late-November night. I almost walked right by the Winnebago. It was parked in an alley. I was walking fast with my head down when I heard Joni Mitchell singing "Big Yellow Taxi." I looked up.

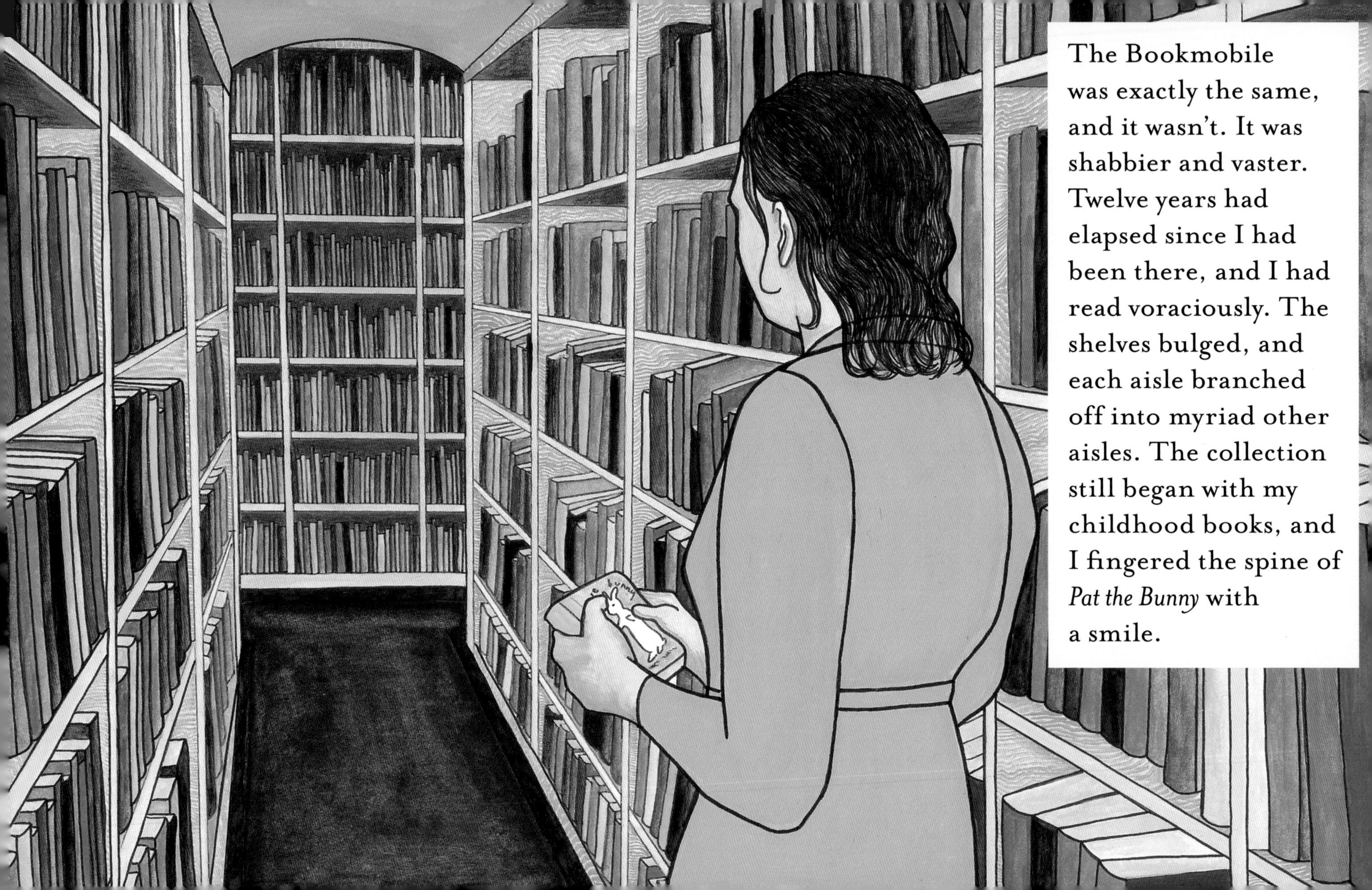

The Bookmobile was exactly the same, and it wasn't. It was shabbier and vaster. Twelve years had elapsed since I had been there, and I had read voraciously. The shelves bulged, and each aisle branched off into myriad other aisles. The collection still began with my childhood books, and I fingered the spine of *Pat the Bunny* with a smile.

Congratulations, Alexandra!

Thank you.

The day before, I had been named director of the Sulzer Library. I wondered how he knew, then realized that he would have cataloged the letter that confirmed my appointment.

Would you care for some tea?

Yes, please.

I drank my tea and explored the farthest recesses of my collection. Each spine was an encapsulated memory, each book represented hours, days of pleasure, of immersion in words. At the very end, on the lowest shelf, was the book I had been reading that morning. I picked it up and opened it. There was my bookmark, but the text continued on, for I had read the book many times. I replaced *The Complete Short Stories of H. G. Wells* on its shelf.

I walked to the front of the Bookmobile. Dawn was still hours away. Mr. Openshaw was leaning on the steering wheel, staring at the cars passing on Western Avenue.

He turned as I approached. I handed him my teacup, and he put it on the dashboard.

Let me come and work for you.

I'm sorry. You don't know what you're asking.

I took my coat from the hook and put it on. I didn't want Mr. Openshaw to see me cry.

I would love to have you at The Library, but the rules don't allow it.

good-bye, Alexandra.

I went home. I still lived in the same apartment I had lived in with Richard. I let myself in, stripped off my wet coat and shoes, and opened my umbrella so it could dry. I walked across the carpet in my socks and stood in the middle of the living room. There were books everywhere. Bookshelves lined the walls. There were piles of books on every table. Heaps of books on the floor. The books had taken over. I thought of everything I had given up for reading. I thought about Richard. I thought about Mr. Openshaw.

"I want to work in the Library."
"You don't know what you're asking."

I found a piece of Chicago Public Library stationery and wrote a note that began, "I'm sorry." I went into the bathroom and looked through the medicine cabinet. I found fourteen Valium tablets. I took them, and then slit my wrists, just in case.

I found myself standing in an immense room: domed, sunlit, beige-carpeted, with shelves and shelves and shelves of books radiating like the spokes of a wheel from the central desk, infinite, with galleries of glass-fronted cases—I was in the Central Reading Room of The Library.

The Library rustled with the sound of thousands of pages being turned. Everywhere I looked, librarians were busy at their tasks, but I didn't see any patrons. Where were the Readers?

I looked down to see if I was bleeding on the carpet, but there were no signs of my recent activities. I was wearing my favorite dress and my most comfortable shoes. My reading glasses hung around my neck. I was wearing the pearl earrings Richard had given me, years ago, in another life.

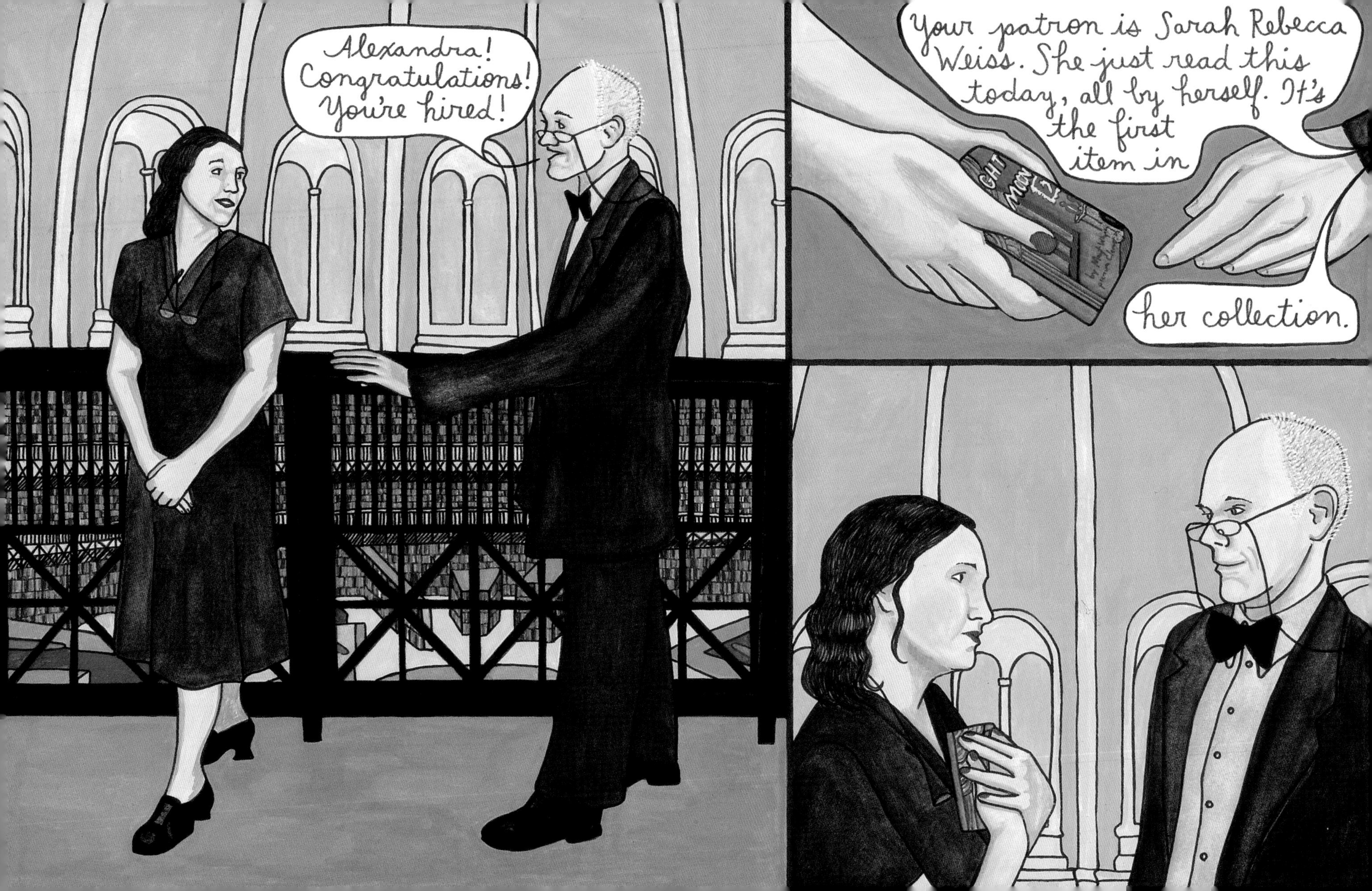
Alexandra! Congratulations! You're hired!
Your patron is Sarah Rebecca Weiss. She just read this today, all by herself. It's the first item in
her collection.

But-
I didn't know how to ask.
Don't worry, Alexandra. They read very slowly at first; you'll get the hang of it long before the volume of acquisitions becomes daunting.
Mr. Openshaw mistook my hesitation.
No—I mean, what about my collection? My Bookmobile?
Oh. Your collection... has been deaccessioned. I was very sorry... But The Library—only living people can be Readers, Alexandra.
My new patron is a young man who is virtually illiterate. His collection is painful to contemplate. But we do what we must.

I looked at the book I was holding. My mother had read it to me over and over until I could read it myself. Good night, good night, good night. Mr. Openshaw was watching me with concern.

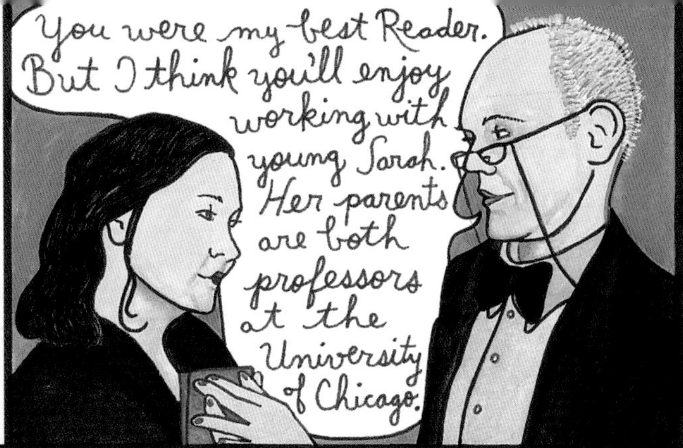
You were my best Reader. But I think you'll enjoy working with young Sarah. Her parents are both professors at the University of Chicago.

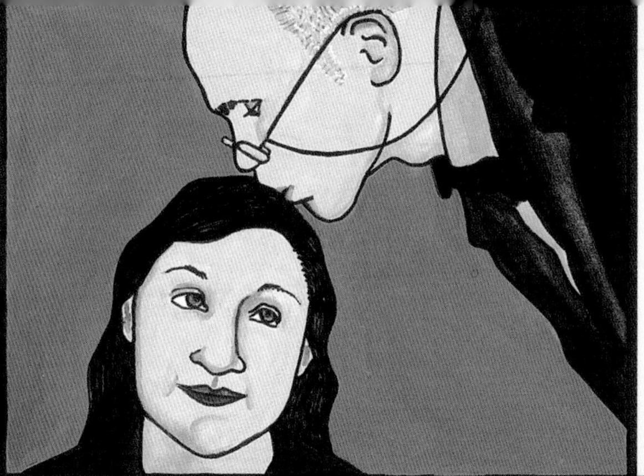

I forced myself to smile. Mr. Openshaw did the same. He gave me a tour of The Library. We had tea in the staff lunchroom. I cataloged *Goodnight Moon*, and placed it all by itself on a shelf in a sparkling new Airstream camper.

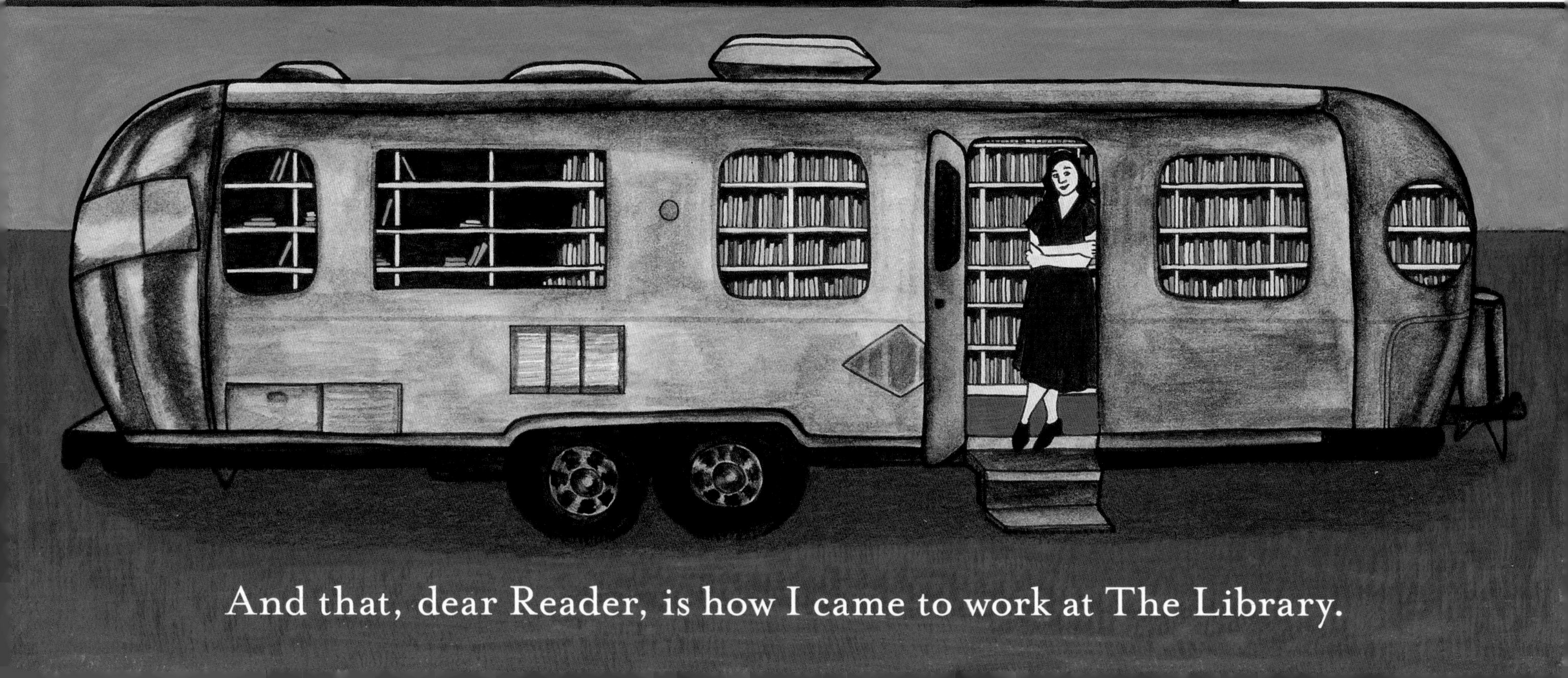
And that, dear Reader, is how I came to work at The Library.

The End

AFTER WORDS

*T*he Night Bookmobile is the first installment of a much larger work, *The Library*, which has its origins in a dream I had as a teenager. I used to die frequently in my dreams, often from causes that should have been insufficient for death, such as touching a doorknob or sneezing. I don't remember how I'd died on this occasion. My dead self was wandering through my grandmother's house (which in reality had many mysterious doors and passages behind the walls), and I discovered a small black door behind the pantry. When I opened the door and squeezed through, I beheld an enormous room filled with stacks of books, comfortable chairs, thick carpet, a piano, long tables with green-shaded lamps that cast little yellow pools of inviting light. It was a library. The ceiling was very high; in fact, where there should have been a ceiling was a distant night sky. The other curious feature of the room was that once I was inside it I ceased to be dead. When I woke up I understood that I had seen a form of heaven.

The Night Bookmobile was more directly inspired by a short story by H. G. Wells, *The Door in the Wall.* In this story a young boy on his way home from school happens to find a door ajar. It leads to a beautiful garden full of playmates and creatures. The boy spends a happy afternoon in the garden and promises to return the next day. But when he arrives home, his father punishes him for lying about the garden. He can't find the door again and eventually grows up and almost forgets it. But then the door begins to appear to him at times when he is unable to enter it. Eventually something tragic happens, and his friends are left to wonder what the door really was, and what their friend thought it was offering him. Heaven? Or something worse?

When I began writing *The Night Bookmobile,* it was a story about a woman's secret life as a reader. As I worked it also became a story about the claims that books place on their readers, the imbalance between our inner and outer lives, a cautionary tale of the seductions of the written word. It became a vision of the afterlife as a library, of heaven as a funky old camper filled with everything you've ever read. What is this heaven? What is it we desire from the hours, weeks, lifetimes we devote to books? What would you sacrifice to sit in that comfy chair with perfect light for an afternoon in eternity, reading the perfect book, forever?

Acknowledgments

I first wrote *The Night Bookmobile* as a short story, which was published in *Zoetrope All Story* in 2004. I adapted it into a serial graphic novel which ran in the London *Guardian*'s Review section from May to December of 2008. I would like to especially thank April Sheridan, who was the model for Alexandra; William Frederick, who was Robert Openshaw; Eric Mandat, who played Richard; and Sharon Britten-Dittmer, who modeled for the Library Patron.

Big thanks are also due to the staff of the Chicago Public Library, particularly Maggie Killacky Jurgenson, who secured the initial permission for me to use the interiors of the

CPL bookmobiles, and to everyone at the Harold Washington Library and the Sulzer

Library who kindly allowed us to shoot reference photos. Many thanks to Lisa Allardice and

Roger Browning at the *Guardian* for inviting me to do the project and for seeing it through

with such panache. Thanks to Jen Thomas for InDesign assistance. And particular thanks

to Michael Ray of *All Story,* who edited the short-story version of *The Night Bookmobile.*

    Thank you to Tamar Brazis at Abrams for her sensitive editing, humor, and patience,

and to Charlie Kochman, Kara Strubel, Michelle Ishay, and Michael Jacobs. Thank you to

Dan Franklin at Jonathan Cape for his willingness to publish crazy beautiful books. Thank

you to Joseph Regal for his sense of adventure, for keeping me sharp, and for making

things happen; thank you to Lauren Schott Pearson, Markus Hoffmann, Michael Strong,

and Barbara Marshall for dealing with the things while they happened.

    Thank you, Dear Reader. Good night, good night.

Published by Jonathan Cape 2010

2 4 6 8 10 9 7 5 3 1

First published in cartoon strip form in the *Guardian*

First published in North America in 2010 by Abrams ComicArts,
an imprint of ABRAMS. All rights reserved.

First published in Great Britain in 2010 by
Jonathan Cape
Random House, 20 Vauxhall Bridge Road,
London SW1V 2SA

www.rbooks.co.uk

Addresses for companies within The Random House Group Limited can be found at:
www.randomhouse.co.uk/offices.htm

The Random House Group Limited Reg. No. 954009

A CIP catalogue record for this book
is available from the British Library

ISBN 9780224089524

The Random House Group Limited makes every effort to ensure that the papers used
in its books are made from trees that have been legally sourced from well-managed
and credibly certified forests. Our paper procurement policy can be found at:
www.randomhouse.co.uk/paper.htm

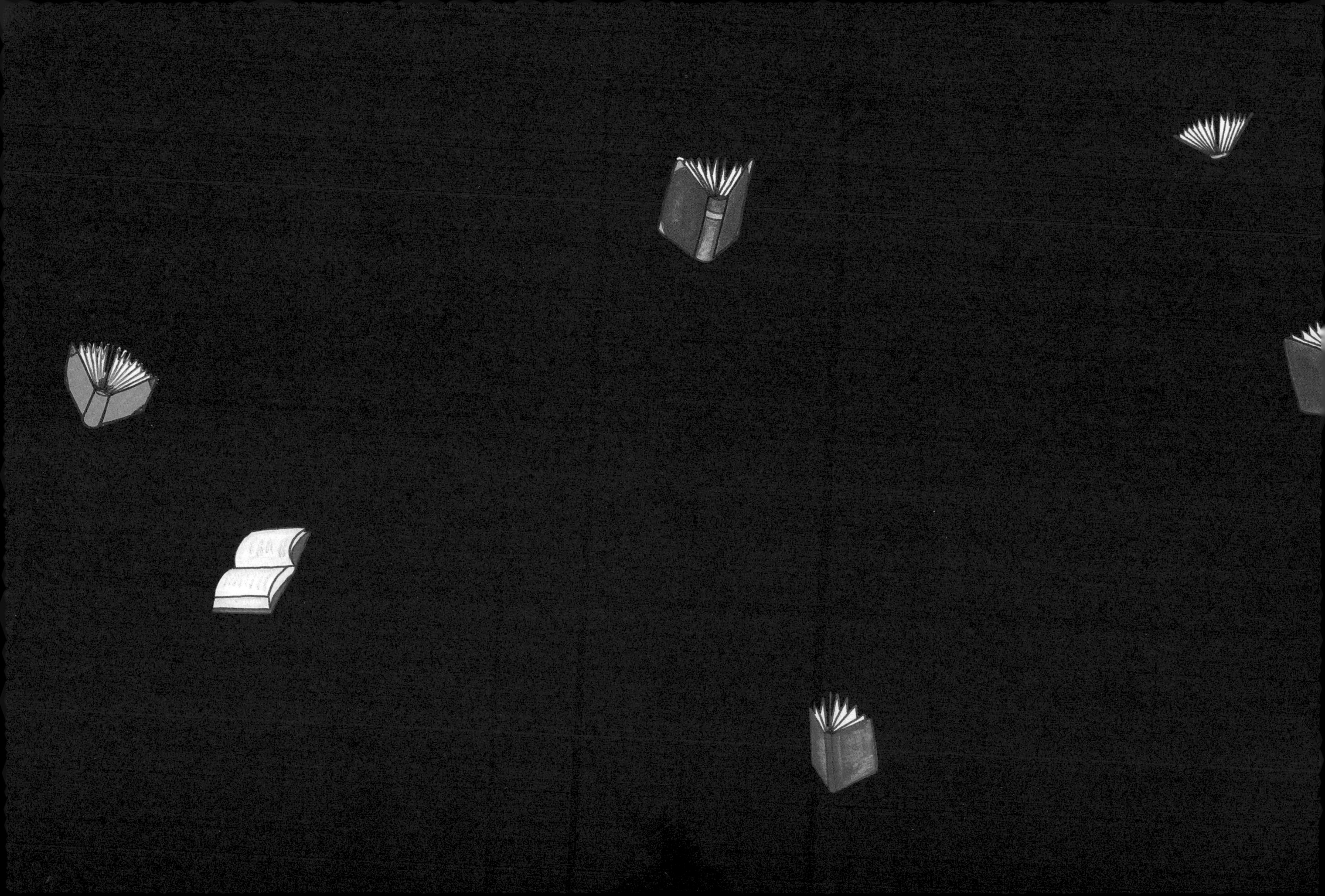